ONE : Minimalism and the Photograph. Radius Books. 2017

Marco Breuer

David Campany

Teju Cole

Thomas Joshua Cooper

Christie Davis

John D'Agata

Michael Fried

John Gossage

Darius Himes

Leah Ollman

Trevor Paglen

Alison Rossiter

Victoria Sambunaris

Laura Steward

Rebecca Norris Webb

James Welling

Perfection is achieved, not when there is nothing more to add, but when there is nothing left to take away.

— ANTOINE DE SAINT-EXUPÉRY

ALISON ROSSITER

LEAH OLLMAN

In Ellsworth Kelly's small collages from the 1950's, I saw the beauty of a simple black placed next to a creamy white, and it reinforced my feeling that photographic tonalities can stand alone as imagery.

— ALISON ROSSITER

Kilborn Acme Kruxo, exact expiration date unknown, ca. 1940, processed 2013, 5 x 7 inches, Gelatin Silver Print, © Alison Rossiter. Courtesy Yossi Milo Gallery, New York

Eyes trace the sloping planes across, down, up; across and down again — the rhythm akin to Rossiter's performance in the dark, sheet in hand, the chemical dip, pour, soak. Slow and silent, the space of this image, its fullness reached by paring away, distilling the photographic to the irreducible ingredient of time.

No camera.

No lens.

No light from the outside world, only the luminosity and darkness latent in the paper itself. No *where* other than the vast intimacy of the page, the tone-scape's deep passage. More than one *when*: the distant death-date stamped on the paper's box, and the immediate sensory rush of such spare, exhilarating beauty.

Breath endures yet on this small, old stage.

— LEAH OLLMAN

TREVOR PAGLEN

LAURA STEWARD

Untitled (Reaper Drone), 2010, C-Print, 48 x 60 inches, © Trevor Paglen. Courtesy the artist

He who is subjected to a field of visibility, and who knows it, assumes responsibility for the constraints of power; he makes them play spontaneously upon himself; he inscribes in himself the power relation in which he simultaneously plays both roles; he becomes the principle of his own subjection.

In 1975 when Michel Foucault wrote these words in his famous book *Discipline and Punish*, he imagined a people pinned by the ever-present eye of the *panopticon*, a term he borrowed from the 18th-century British philosopher Jeremy Bentham. Bentham designed a circular institutional building with an observation tower at its center, the panopticon, like the hub of a wheel. The design was such that guards could easily see out of the tower, but inmates could not see in, and thus could not tell when they were being observed. Foucault surmised that the inmates would internalize their own observation.

Drones, like the one in Trevor Paglen's photograph, did not yet exist when Foucault adopted the monolithic and all-seeing panopticon as a metaphor for state surveillance. Today the metaphor of the monolithic tower has been replaced, but not with a metaphor. Technological change has exploded the panopticon into millions of shards in the years since Foucault wrote. Those shards are not metaphors, they are drones.

Foucault wrote that to be observed by the panopticon was to be "the object of information, never a subject in communication." In his photographs, Paglen observes the observer, becomes a subject rather than an object. It's the observational equivalent of a riot in Jeremy Bentham's prison.

— LAURA STEWARD

JAMES WELLING

MICHAEL FRIED

Lamp, Vals, 2013, Inkjet Print, 15 x 10 inches. © James Welling. Courtesy the artist and David Zwirner, New York/London

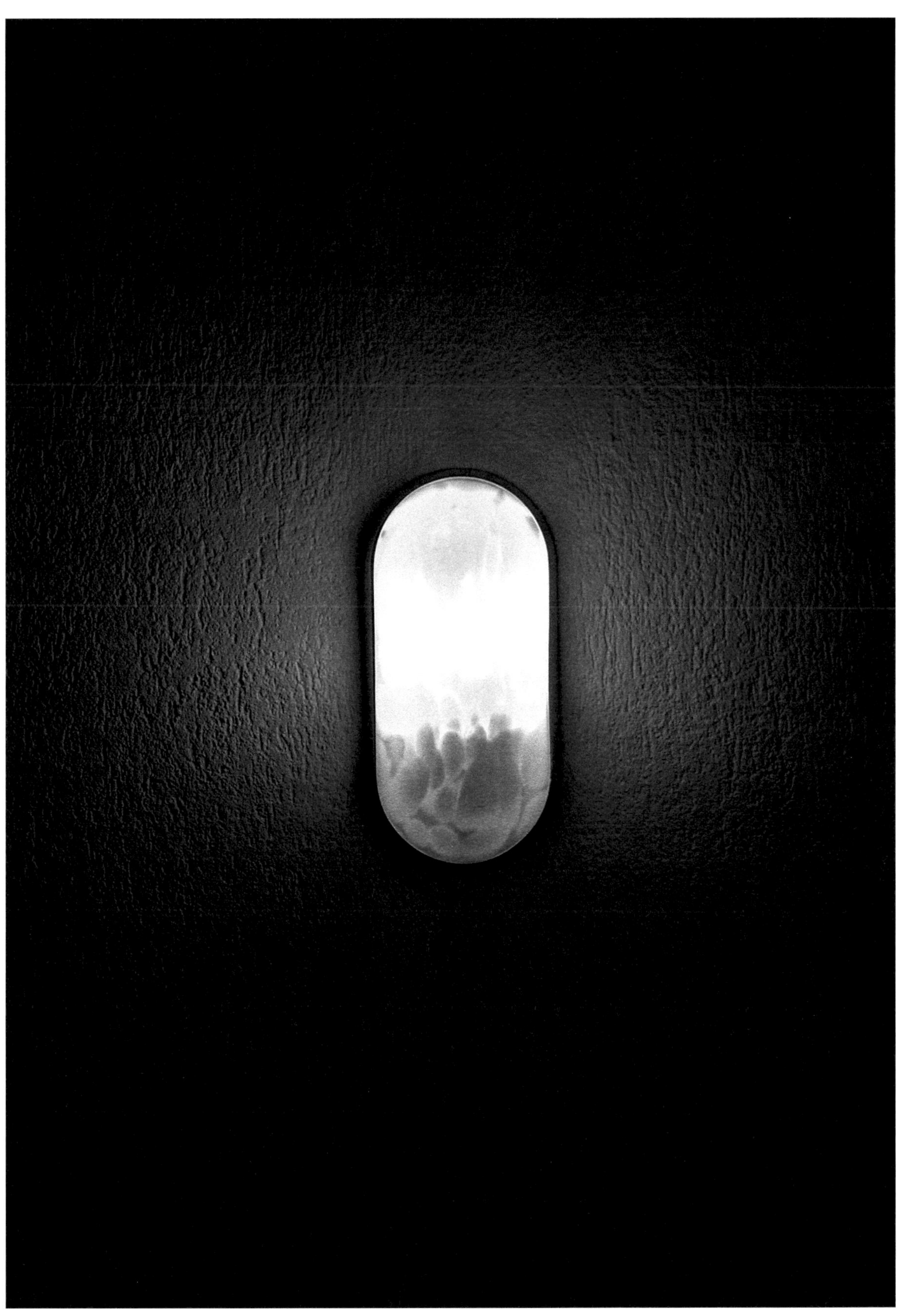

The Rest

I google Ian's dates
and see that he died thirteen years ago.
It doesn't seem possible —
all those cigarettes unsmoked,
all those bottles of wine
gone unsummoned at the end of meals
to pour one more glass, or half a glass,
and leave the rest.

— MICHAEL FRIED

JOHN GOSSAGE

DAVID CAMPANY

What we, or at any rate I, refer to confidently as memory-meaning a moment, a scene, a fact that has been subjected to a fixative and thereby rescued from oblivion — is really a form of storytelling that goes on continually in the mind and often changes with the telling. Too many conflicting emotional interests are involved for life ever to be wholly acceptable, and possibly it is the work of the storyteller to rearrange things so that they conform to this end. In any case, in talking about the past we lie with every breath we draw.

– WILLIAM MAXWELL

Arlington, Virginia, 2012, Silver Gelatin Prints.

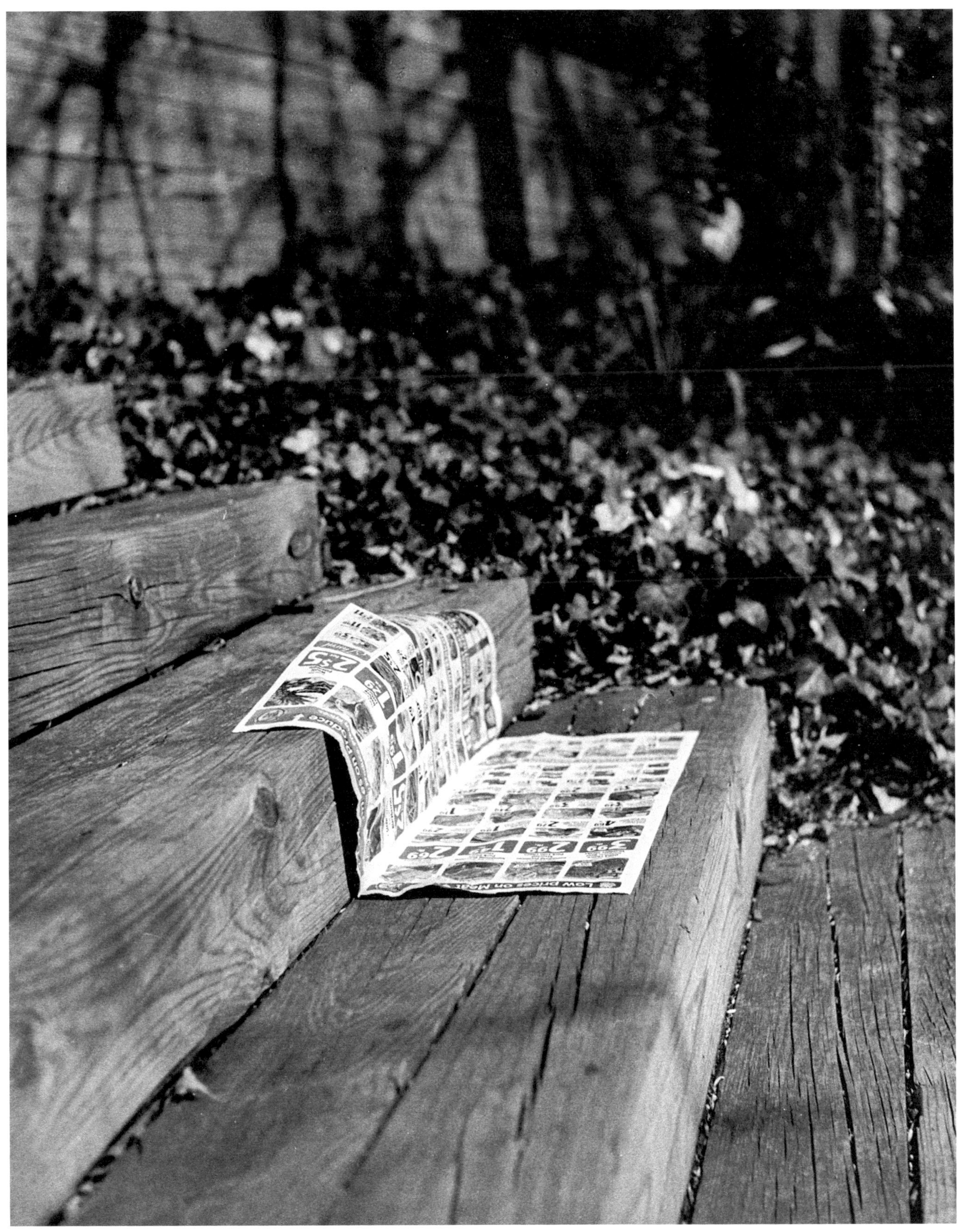

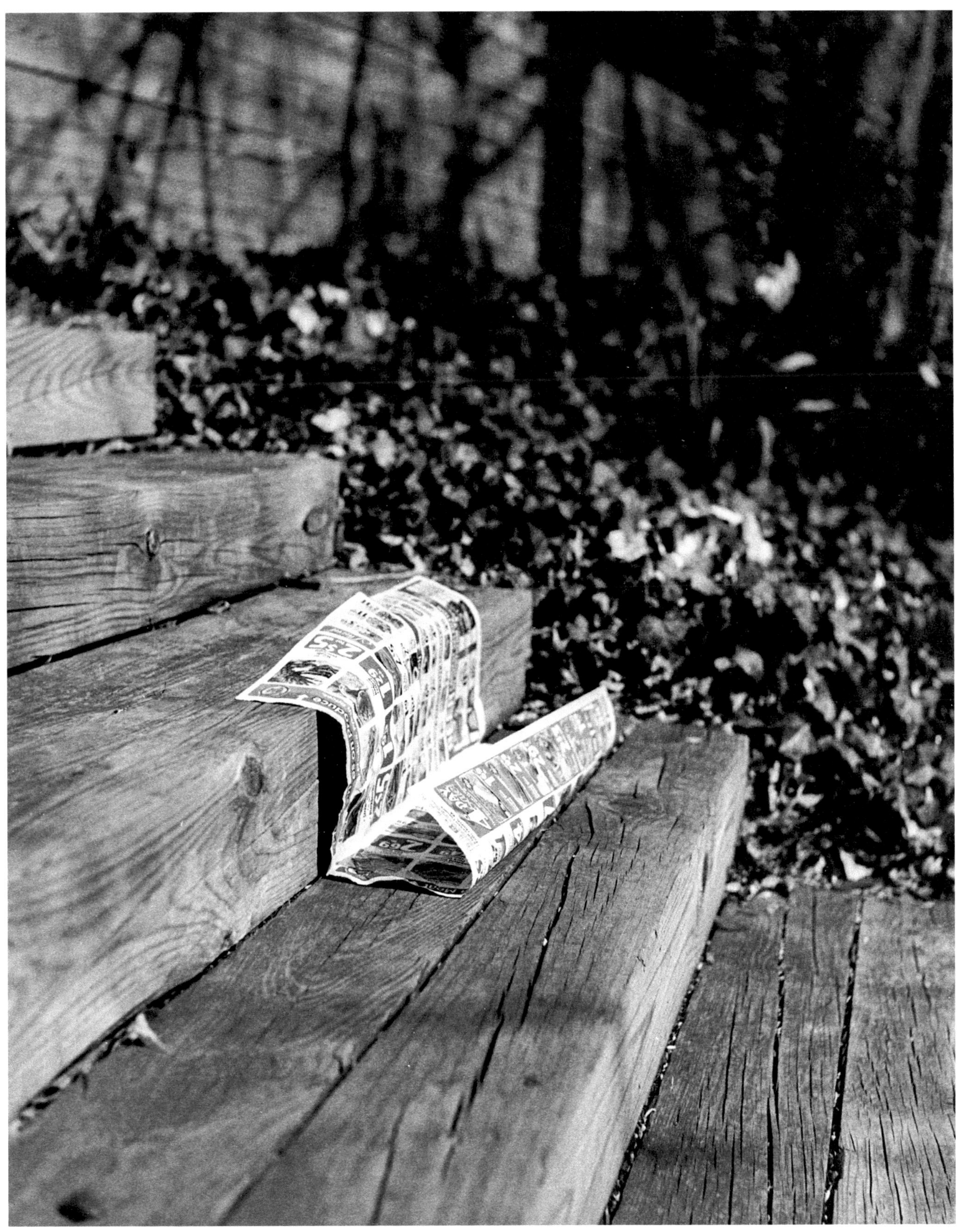

Minimal | Maximal

Look through the viewfinder and your frame is already full.
Open the shutter and the rays will flood in, hitting that light sensitive surface at once, all over.
An excess of fact. Quite maximal.
Such excess, chaos even, is your raw material, your resource. A frame forces selection from it.
This is in, that is out. A shutter asks for this moment, not that. The lens and aperture allow focus upon something, everything, or nothing.
These actions are subtractive. While not minimal, they tend toward it.

——

Every artist continually wants to reach the edge of nothingness — the point where you can't go any further.

HARRY CALLAHAN, PHOTOGRAPHER

——

For a contemporary painter the blank canvas and the monochrome loom large on the horizon of possibility. Once accepted as artistic gestures and legitimate works of art, every painting thereafter becomes a painting on a painting.
Similar paths do exist for photography (the unexposed/overexposed frame or print, or monochromes made by a variety of means).
What would it mean if the first exercise for a student of photography was to make a print from an unexposed negative and then a print from a totally overexposed one? Would it be no more than an exercise, a hoop to jump through? Or would it ground an understanding of photography upon something else, something set apart from the weighty presumptions of depiction?

——

Photography's paths to the minimal need not resemble what the minimal is for painting.
A photograph quickly taken might be minimal.
A photograph of a plain façade of a building might be minimal.
A figure in the center of the frame might be minimal.
A single fork on a table.
A sheet of newsprint in the wind.

——

Photography has scrambled the old hierarchies of genre and subject matter. It has mixed major and minor. It has debased the monarch (once snapped, 'The Queen' becomes a queen) and it has elevated trash.
The monarch and the trash can tell you all you need know about some societies.

——

Charles Baudelaire noted that while a cobbler who makes a good pair of shoes today can be fairly confident in making a good pair tomorrow, a poet who writes a good poem today has no such guarantee. A good society needs good shoes and good poems. While Baudelaire liked trash, he did not like photography, which is generally akin to shoe-making although sometimes to poetry.
But it does complicate the distinction.

——

— DAVID CAMPANY

THOMAS JOSHUA COOPER

CHRISTIE DAVIS

Fading Moonlight. Looking Toward the Tropic of Cancer, The Gulf of Mexico. Tepehuajes. Tamaulipas. Mexico, 2007/2015, Latin North America, Silver Gelatin Print, 40 x 60 inches. Courtesy the artist

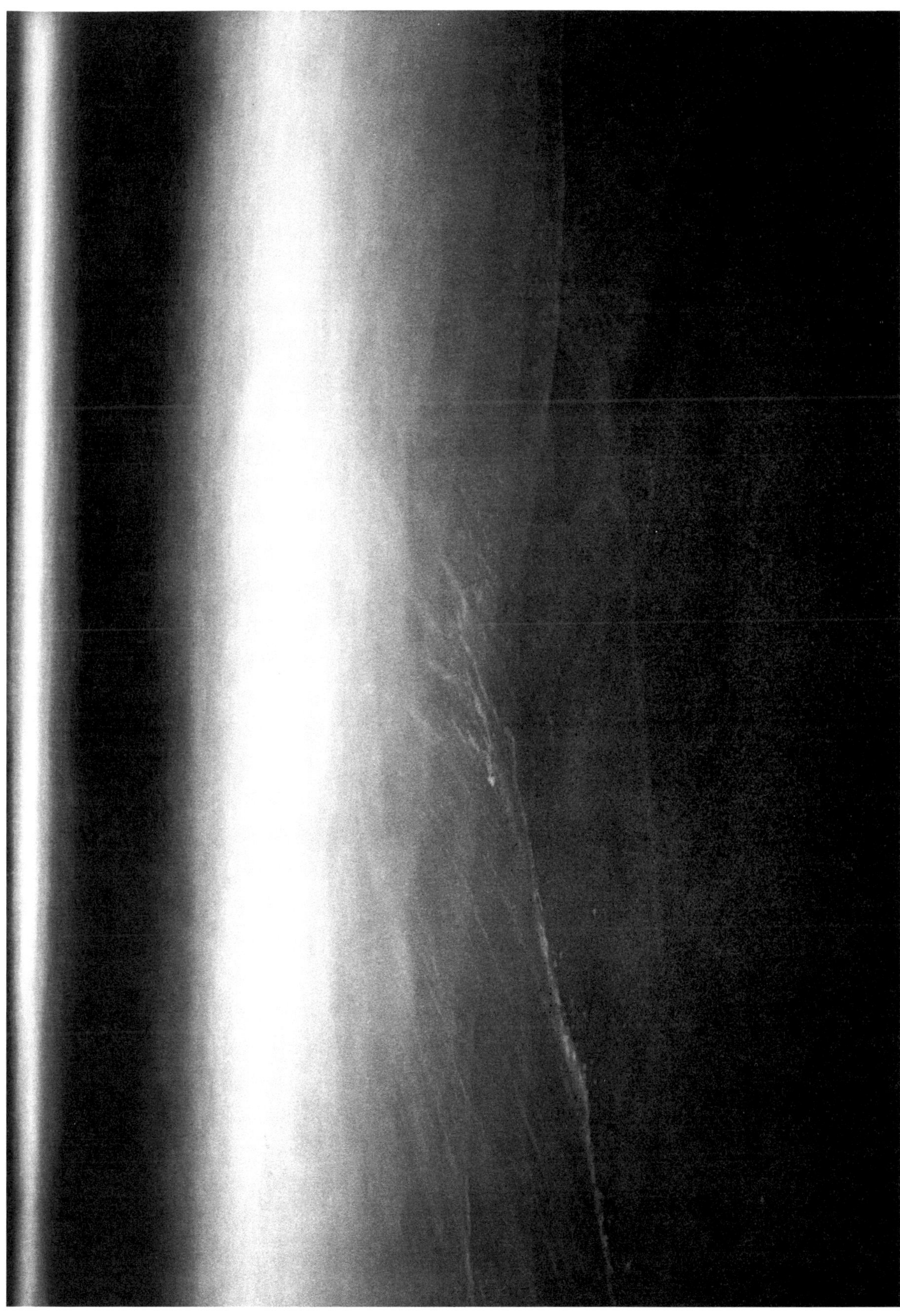

I am involved in the making and assembly of a large, thematic body of work, that is developed out of the physical act of visually and pictorially mapping the cardinal extremes immensely described as the Atlantic Basin.

—THOMAS JOSHUA COOPER

I, Jerónimo de Aguilar, look at the New World before closing my eyes forever, and the last thing I see is the coast of Veracruz and the ships setting sail filled with Mexican treasure, guided by the most trustworthy of compasses: a sun of gold and a moon of silver, both simultaneously hanging over a blue-black sky that is stormy on high but bloody as soon as it touches the surface of the water.

—CARLOS FUENTES "THE TWO SHORES"

Following in the footsteps of European explorers, from the Norwegian Viking Erik the Red to Spanish conquistador Hernán Cortés, Thomas Joshua Cooper became a modern-day explorer in the process of making his *Atlas of Emptiness and Extremity*. As an American living in Europe for the last 40 years, he found himself looking back across the Atlantic and wondering what led these men to take such a leap into the unknown. Unlike the explorers before him, he brings no weapons, no disease, no violent hand. Rather he is armed with wonder and patience and his 1898 Agfa field camera. And he takes nothing from these places or their people except photographs.

As imagined by Carlos Fuentes, we hear testament from the ghost of a Franciscan friar who, as a translator along with La Malinche, assisted Cortés with the 1519 Spanish conquest of Mexico and the swift destruction of the Aztec Empire. In Cooper's picture it is that same "moon of silver" we see shining on the Gulf of Mexico nearly 500 years later.

— CHRISTIE DAVIS

VICTORIA SAMBUNARIS

JOHN D'AGATA

Is it that by its indefiniteness it shadows forth the heartless voids and immensities of the universe, and thus stabs us from behind with the thought of annihilation, when beholding the white depths of the milky way? Or is it, that as in essence whiteness is not so much a color as the visible absence of color, and at the same time the concrete of all colors; is it for these reasons that there is such a dumb blankness, full of meaning, in a wide landscape of snows — a colorless, all-color of atheism from which we shrink?

— HERMAN MELVILLE

Untitled (White Trains on Salt Flats, I–80) Great Salt Lake Desert Utah, 2002, Chromogenic Print. 39 x 55 inches © Victoria Sambunaris. Courtesy of Yancey Richardson Gallery, New York

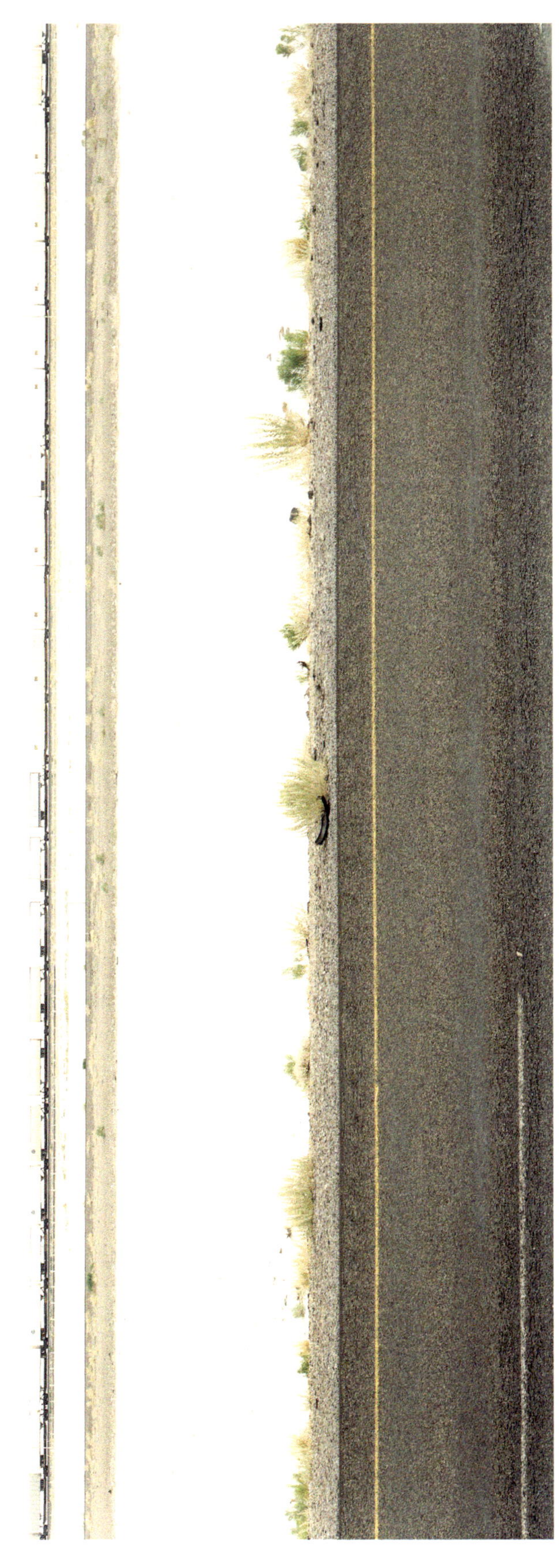

On Vicky's White

Herman Melville published *Moby-Dick* in the middle of the 19th century, at the height of the largest influx of immigrants to America.

Prior to then however, any increase in the population was fueled by families that had already been living in America for at least a few generations. Between 1770 and 1830, for example, census data suggests that there was hardly any immigration at all. Six thousand people in 1780; 7,500 in 1800; 8,000 in 1820.

But then, something happened. Famines in Europe, cheap land in the Midwest, a gold rush in Idaho, Arizona, Kansas, and California. By 1830 immigration in the U.S. increased to 140,000 people. A decade later it quadrupled to 600,000 people. And by 1850 it tripled once more, totaling 1.7 million. In less than a generation the foreign-born population of the United States went from 1.5% to more than 10%. And those who considered themselves "native-born" Americans were threatened by the influx.

The American Party was founded in the 1850s in order to fight immigration politically, while everyday Americans staged their own violent protests in states across the U.S.—from the burning of a Catholic orphanage in Bangor, Maine, to the largest mass lynching in American history in New Orleans.

It was during this period that P. T. Barnum's American Museum in New York City was at the height of its popularity. During its twenty-five-year run in the mid-1800s, the museum sold 45 million tickets—roughly 44 million more tickets than there were even people in New York.

He sold to both the lower class and the upper class, to "native borns" and recent immigrants, and at a time when different races seldom mixed in American society Barnum also sold tickets to both blacks and whites. In many ways, the American Museum transcended difference while simultaneously exploiting the exoticness of "others" through a hodgepodge of exhibits of tattooed children, acrobatic fleas, minstrel shows, ventriloquists, contortionists, magicians, a mermaid, a white whale, a lady with a beard, and a tree under which—it was claimed on a plaque—Jesus' disciples once sat.

Nothing else like it had ever existed in America.

This was a time when there were few parks in the country—nor beaches, sports teams, concert halls, etc. The average American worked at least six days a week, so even the idea of "weekends" was alien to most. Which is why Barnum's museum uniquely promoted an individual's right to explore his curiosity about the grotesque and sublime: at 2 o'clock a performance of Shakespeare's *Othello*; at 4 o'clock an exhibition of Cheng and Eng, the Siamese twins.

When it was destroyed by a fire in 1865, an editorial in *The Nation* magazine bid farewell to Barnum's. "We desire to give the American Museum all the credit it deserves, for it needs it all," the editorial began, before going on to propose a new museum for the city of New York, an institution more fitting for "a first-class city," committed to the "seriousness" and "sobriety" of natural history—botany, zoology, geology, mineralogy—the myriad specializations that were beginning to emerge as the 19th century sought to carve up the world into easily knowable substrata of meanings:

> *It is one thing to love shells and minerals, and to enjoy collections of them, but quite another to enjoy every collection of them. The more truly one loves a collection well arranged, the more he will be offended by a chaotic, dusty, dishonored collection. The more one loves the order and system of scientific enquiry, the more he will feel personally injured by disorder and a lack of system among the materials of scientific enquiry. . . . Without scientific arrangement, without a catalogue, without attendants, without even labels, in most respects, the heterogeneous heap of curiosities, valuable and worthless mixed together, could not attract serious visitors very often enough to detain them long.*

What P. T. Barnum understood however is that the "valuable" and the "worthless," when mixed together, can inspire one to find brand new meanings of one's own. From the Greek word *mouseion*—"the home of the Muses"—museums have always been a place for amusement, music, and musing, a space in which one can get lost in one's thoughts, wandering between ideas both grotesque and sublime.

This might be the era in American culture when the word "scientist" was coined, but it was also when the term "haute couture" was introduced, when Lewis Carroll published *Alice's Adventures in Wonderland*, when a bike-riding frenzy overtook the U.S., and when we first read that intimately fateful opening sentence "Call me Ishmael," and felt ourselves compelled into service to help unravel those two complex strands in Herman Melville's *Moby-Dick*: the voyage of the *Pequod* to kill the whale, and Ishmael's own voyage to make sense of that adventure.

"Some years ago, never mind how long precisely," Ishmael continues in the second sentence of the book, signaling to us with his very next breath which of those two voyages will really matter in this book: Never mind how long precisely.

This is a book that wanders, that muses, that uses facts and information to help expand its curiosity, rather than to dictate the limits of ours.

"We can hypothesize," Ishmael tells us at one point in the book, "even if we cannot prove and establish." And so while Captain Ahab drives toward a triumphant end to his quest, Ishmael revels in the endless minutiae of cetology, the hieroglyphic significance of the scars on Moby's body, an analysis of a painting in the Spouter Inn, and a meditation on the meaning of the color white. As many scholars have explained, Ishmael's proclivity for interpreting everything comes close to exhausting the very virtues of interpretation.

Yet what we eventually realize, thanks to Ishmael's doggedness, is that with so many possible interpretations in the world, perhaps there is no single "right" way to see anything, perhaps more than one answer might exist to a question, perhaps white looks empty and vacuous and void of any meaning, but is secretly a conflagration of all the other colors—that place on the spectrum where all light has merged.

— JOHN D'AGATA

MARCO BREUER

DARIUS HIMES

List for *Untitled (C–1787)*

absence (vs. presence), abstraction; **c**hance (vs. control), color, conventions (of the medium); **d**rawing; **e**mulsion, entropy, erasure, extraction; **f**ailure (degrees of), figure (vs. ground), flow, force, form (human), found, Fox Talbot (W.H.), freehand, Frisch (Max); **g**esture; **h**and, Handke (Peter); **I** (self), iconoclasm, internal/external; line; **m**aterial, (deliberate) misuse, movement, mutability; **n**egative, negotiation, nothing; **o**bject (vs. window); **p**arameters, perception, performance, personal (vs. private), photographic, plane, positive, preliminary, process, provisional; **q**uestion; **s**hadow, shape, *Silent Speed*, silhouette, simplicity, space, stack, subtraction; **t**ool, trace, translation; **v**ariant, void, volume.

— MARCO BREUER

Untitled (C-1787), 2016, Chromogenic Paper, exposed/embossed/scraped

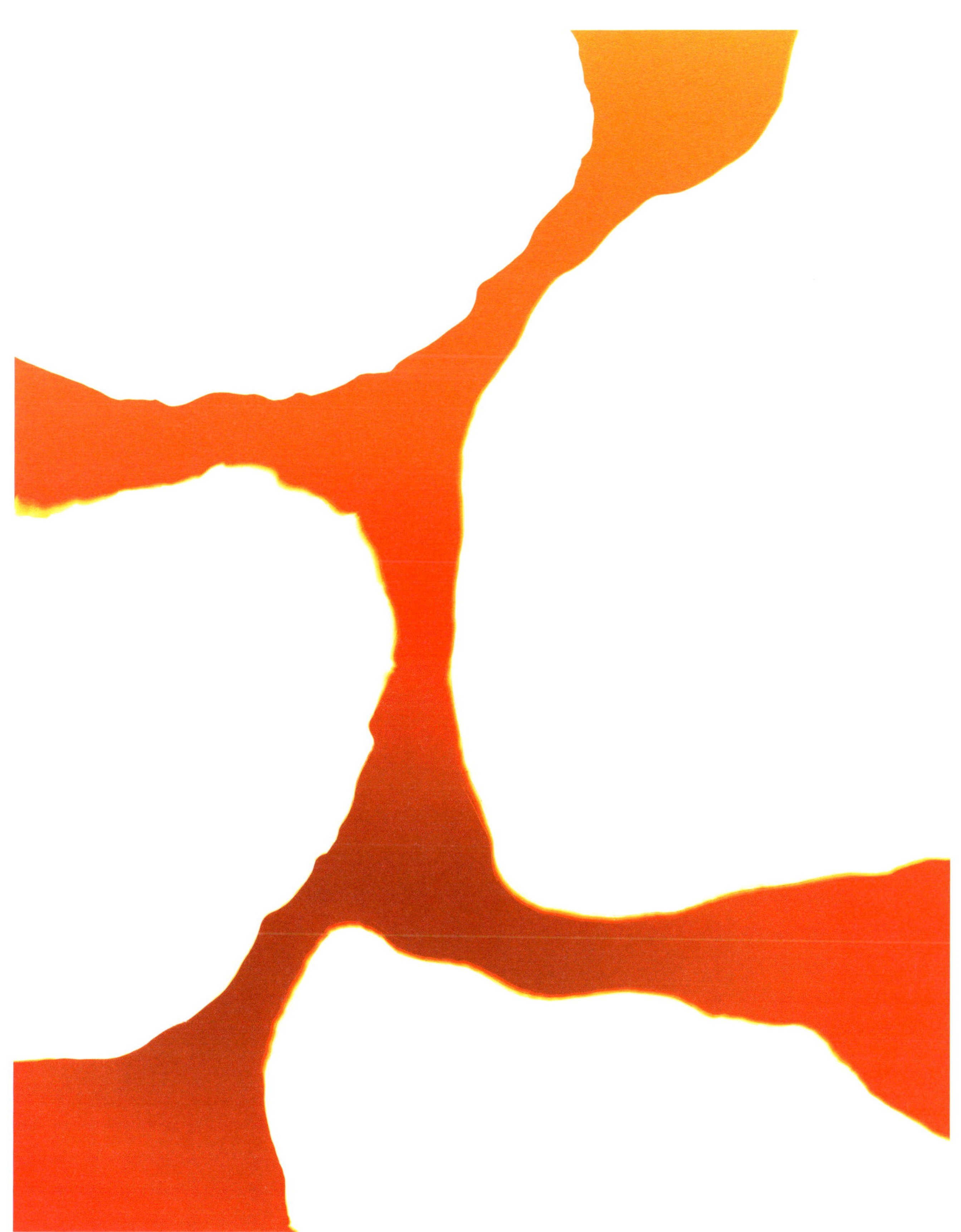

Playing with 'gangs of kosmos,' pushing and pulling light with a flirtatious banter of absence and presence, Breuer is both priest and supplicant, praying and prostrating in his darkroom temple, finding his 'inspiration in real objects to-day,' as Whitman prophesied. How magical is a photograph?! Standing as a ready and willing participant in unveiling mystery, it literally captures light and transfixes it! What?! How?! Is this true?!

Each sheet of paper is Breuer's blank canvas; setting aside the camera and lens, he opts for a pure, raw, new visual language, markings made in collaboration with light itself. Beauty, existence and being, justice, judgments on perfection, a knowledge and reasoning about the Universal—all these currents cycle through and circle around his works. The results are both questions and answers, willed into existence.

— DARIUS HIMES

REBECCA NORRIS WEBB

TEJU COLE

Teju Cole : *Zürich,* 2014, Archival Pigment Print, 20 x 27.5 inches. Courtesy of the artist

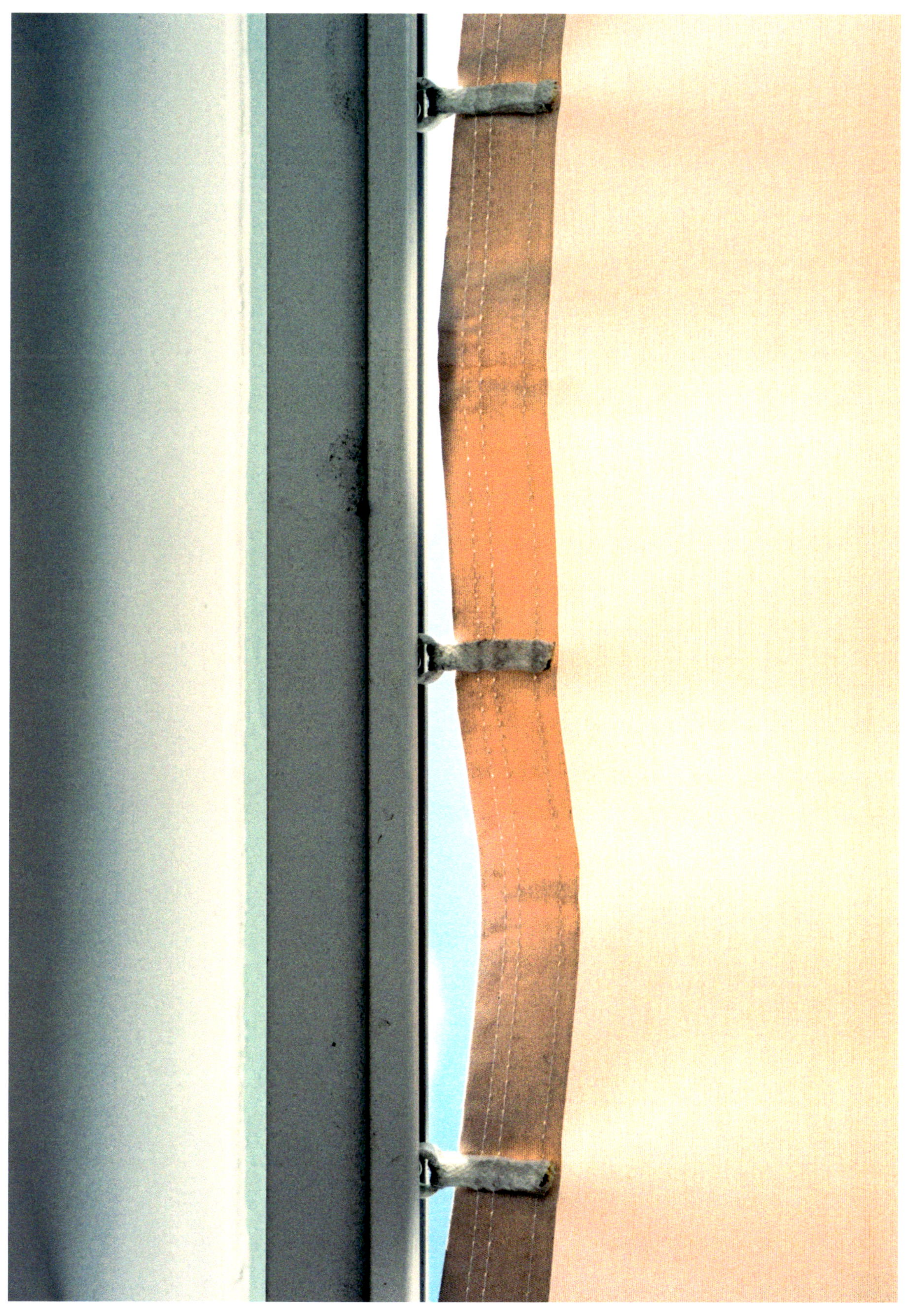

A length, a line. A curve, a cut that reveals the inner air. Faraway wave seen from the deck of the ship. I think the Annunciation must have happened on a day like this one.

— TEJU COLE

Blue River Road. All it takes is one good rain to become a river again. Is that why you taught me to float before I could swim?

— REBECCA NORRIS WEBB

Rebecca Norris Webb : *Floodplain,* 2016. Chromogenic Print, 20 x 30 inches, ed. of 10. Courtesy of Ricco/Maresca Gallery, NY; Robert Klein Gallery, Boston; Robert Koch Gallery, San Francisco

ACKNOWLEDGMENTS

The initial idea for this book was to publish only a very small edition — one that would coincide with Radius Books' participation in Paris Photo. That edition launched in late 2016 and comprised only 150 signed and numbered copies. The text pages were printed in Italy; the photographs were printed in the U.S. by Michael Lundgren as archival pigment prints; the copies were assembled in Santa Fe, a process made necessary by the fact that every image was tipped into the book by hand.

The project was conceived as a sketch of sorts. It was quickly — albeit lovingly — produced, and our approach was to give both the photographers and writers freedom to play with the topic of minimalism and photography in whatever way they chose. The results exceeded our expectations: smart, readable, and while small in scale and scope, also very complex and nuanced.

We felt compelled to share this work with a larger audience, and so this edition, at a slightly reduced size, a much reduced price, and more traditional printing and binding, is meant to give more people a chance to read and hold the results. It has been produced in a quantity of 1500 copies, printed on 150gsm Garda Bianka paper, and will be donated to the entire network of schools and libraries in our Donation Program.

This project would not have been possible without inspiration and guidance from Darius Himes and Lucas Zwirner in the early planning stages. The incredible printing in both editions is due to the time and hard work that Michael Lundgren put into the image files. Neither edition would have happened without the incredible support of Patrick Lannan and Christie Davis at the Lannan Foundation.